WITHDRAWN

A Picture Book of
Samuel Adams

A Picture Book of Samuel Adams

by David A. Adler and Michael S. Adler
illustrated by Ronald Himler

Holiday House / New York

For Deborah, with love
M. S. A.

For Myra and Bob
R. H.

Text copyright © 2005 by David A. Adler and Michael S. Adler
Illustrations copyright © 2005 by Ronald Himler
All Rights Reserved
Printed in the United States of America
www.holidayhouse.com
First Edition
1 3 5 7 9 10 8 6 4 2

Library of Congress Cataloging-in-Publication Data
Adler, David A.
A picture book of Samuel Adams / by David A. Adler and Michael S. Adler ;
illustrated by Ronald Himler.— 1st ed.
p. cm.
Includes bibliographical references.
ISBN 0-8234-1846-4
1. Adams, Samuel, 1722–1803—Juvenile literature.
2. Politicians—United States—Biography—Juvenile literature.
3. United States. Declaration of Independence—Signers—Biography—Juvenile literature.
4. United States—History—Revolution, 1775–1783—Juvenile literature.
I. Adler, Michael S. II. Himler, Ronald. III. Title.

E302.6.A2A38 2005
973.3'13'092—dc22
[B]
2004049346

Samuel Adams was an American patriot, a firebrand.
"Every dip of his pen," one Englishman said of him,
"stung like a horned snake." His letters, essays, and
speeches pushed the thirteen American colonies
toward revolution.

Samuel Adams was born on September 27, 1722, in Boston, Massachusetts. He was one of twelve children of Mary and Samuel "Deacon" Adams. Health care was primitive in the 1700s and many babies did not survive. Only three of the Adams children—Samuel, Mary, and Joseph—lived to be adults.

The Adams family lived in a large house next to their brewery. Young Samuel often sat on a rooftop platform of the house and watched sailors load and unload ships in nearby Boston Harbor.

Samuel's mother taught him to read and write, and at the age of six, his parents sent him to the Boston Grammar School.

Samuel was a good student and loved to learn. "The value of learning exceeds riches," he wrote in the margin of one of his books. At the age of fourteen he entered Harvard College. He studied history and philosophy. He soon had strong feelings about the rights of people to govern themselves, and he headed toward a life in politics.

In 1743 Samuel Adams was awarded an advanced degree from Harvard. The royal governor of Massachusetts was there when Adams gave his graduation speech. Even then, long before the Revolutionary War, Adams spoke about a people's right to oppose their king.

After school, Adams worked in a Boston bank, but he spent too much time talking politics and too little time banking. He soon lost his job. His father gave him money to start his own business, but Adams lent most of it to a friend who never repaid him. Next Adams went to work in his father's brewery, but again he spent more time talking politics than working.

In 1747 Adams and some of his friends started a newspaper, the *Public Advertiser.* In the first issue he attacked the local British government.

On October 17, 1749, Samuel married Elizabeth Checkley, a minister's daughter.

Samuel and Elizabeth had six children, but only two—Samuel and Hannah—lived beyond their first few months. On July 25, 1758, shortly after a tragic pregnancy, Elizabeth died.

In 1764 Samuel married Elizabeth "Betsy" Wells. One of Betsy and Samuel's wedding gifts was Surry, a household slave. Adams didn't believe in slavery and immediately freed her. Surry chose to remain with Betsy and Samuel Adams and work for them as a free woman.

Betsy Adams had no children of her own, but she helped to raise her stepchildren, young Samuel and Hannah.

In 1755 fighting had broken out in America between the English and the French—the beginning of the French and Indian War. The fighting didn't end until 1763.

To help pay the cost of this war, the English Parliament imposed new taxes on the American colonies. The Sugar Act of 1764 was a tax on molasses. The Stamp Act of 1765 put a tax on all printing goods sold in the American colonies.

There was no representative from the American colonies in Parliament. That moved James Otis, a member of the Massachusetts Assembly, to declare, "Taxation without representation is tyranny."

At town meetings Adams also spoke out against the taxes. He wrote angry letters to newspapers and helped like-minded men organize themselves into a group called the Sons of Liberty.

The men met outdoors, under an elm they called the Liberty Tree. On August 13, 1765, they hung a dummy from the tree with a picture of a British tax agent on it. To show their hatred of Lord Bute, the king's adviser, they hung a giant boot. The next night the Sons of Liberty threw stones through the windows of the tax agent's house and destroyed his office.

In September 1765 Adams was elected to the Massachusetts Assembly. There he joined James Otis. Together, they helped organize the October 1765 Stamp Act Congress.

Adams couldn't attend the congress, but delegates from nine colonies did. They met in New York and declared November 1, the day the tax would become law, a day of fasting and mourning.

The protests worked. Early in 1766 Parliament repealed the Stamp Act. When the news reached Boston, a crowd gathered around the Liberty Tree and celebrated with rockets, candles, and banners.

The English government was still in debt, so in 1767 Parliament passed the Townshend Acts, taxes on glass, lead, paper, paint, and tea.

Adams and other patriots fought the Townshend Acts. Most of the patriots only wanted to end the taxes, but by 1769 Adams was calling to end the king's rule in the colonies.

Resistance began to grow against British rule.
The people of Boston hated having British soldiers,
or redcoats as they called them, in their city.

On March 5, 1770, a group of colonists shouted at some redcoats, and threw snow and chunks of ice. The soldiers shot and killed five men in what was later called the Boston Massacre.

Just after the "massacre," Adams joined a committee to get the British troops out of Boston. "It is at your peril if you do not," he told the lieutenant governor. Within a week of the incident, the troops were moved from the center of the city.

During these difficult times, Adams wrote letters to people in other colonies to let them know what was happening in Boston. In 1772, at a town meeting, he organized the first Committee of Correspondence to declare the rights of the people of Massachusetts and to keep in touch with patriots in other colonies.

In November 1773 three British ships loaded with tea docked in Boston Harbor. Patriots told the royal governor to send the ships back to England. The governor refused.

On December 16, the day before the ships were to be unloaded, Adams and thousands of other patriots met in Boston. They sent a messenger to the governor again asking to send the ships away. When the governor didn't respond, Adams announced, "This meeting can do nothing more to save the country!"

After Adams spoke, members of the Sons of Liberty boarded the ships, broke open 342 chests of tea, and dumped them into the harbor. This act of defiance, soon called the Boston Tea Party, led directly to the Revolutionary War.

When news of the "party" reached England, members of Parliament were furious. First they voted to close Boston Harbor. Later they outlawed town meetings and forced colonists to let redcoats live in their homes.

In September 1774 Samuel Adams and more than fifty other delegates from twelve colonies met in Philadelphia at the First Continental Congress to discuss their problems with England. They sent a message of protest to Parliament. They also decided to gather weapons in case of war.

The British felt it was time to stop the rebels.

On April 18, 1775, General Thomas Gage, the commander of British troops in America, sent hundreds of redcoats to destroy weapons hidden in Concord, Massachusetts. From there they were to march to nearby Lexington and arrest Samuel Adams and John Hancock. Gage planned to send the two patriots to England where they would be tried for treason.

Two Sons of Liberty, Paul Revere and William Dawes, rode from Boston. Revere arrived in Lexington sometime past midnight on the morning of April 19. He warned Adams and Hancock, who escaped into the woods. Later, Revere was stopped in Lexington by the British. Dawes fell from his horse, but another man, Samuel Prescott, rode ahead to Concord and alerted the patriots there.

At about dawn the first shots of the Revolution were fired. Adams watched from a hill and said, "What a glorious morning for America is this!"

General Gage hoped the patriots would give up their revolt. In June he offered to pardon the men who had taken up arms against his redcoats, all except Adams and Hancock. He called them arch-traitors and promised a reward to anyone who captured them, but no one did.

Adams represented Massachusetts at the Second Continental Congress in Philadelphia. He signed the Declaration of Independence in 1776. Adams helped write the Articles of Confederation, the rules that governed the United States until 1789, when the Constitution became the foundation of the government.

Early in 1781 Adams went home. He stayed near Boston for the rest of his life.

In 1783 the British signed a peace treaty and recognized the new nation, the United States of America.

Samuel Adams kept busy with Massachusetts politics. In 1782 he was elected to the state senate. In 1789, when John Hancock was elected governor of Massachusetts, Adams was elected lieutenant governor. Four years later Hancock died and Adams became governor.

In 1796 John Adams, Samuel's cousin, ran for president, but Samuel did not support him. John Adams was a Federalist, a believer in a strong central government. Samuel supported his opponent, Thomas Jefferson, who wanted more power left with the states and the people.

John Adams became president in 1797, but was defeated by Jefferson in the next election. By then Samuel Adams was an old man. His health was failing. In January 1797 he retired from public life.

On October 2, 1803, with his wife, Elizabeth, at his side, Samuel Adams died. He was eighty-one.

Samuel Adams had worked to see his dream of an independent, democratic American nation come true. For all he did he is often called the Father of the Revolution.

IMPORTANT DATES

1722	Born in Boston, September 27.
1743	Awarded a master's degree by Harvard College.
1749	Marries Elizabeth Checkley, October 17.
1751	Son, Samuel, born.
1756	Daughter, Hannah, born.
1758	Elizabeth Checkley Adams dies, July 25.
1764	Marries Elizabeth "Betsy" Wells, December 6.
1765	Stamp Act protests in Boston, August 13 and 14.
1766	Stamp Act repealed, February 22.
1770	Boston Massacre, March 5.
1773	Boston Tea Party, December 16.
1775	First battles of the Revolution at Lexington and Concord, Massachusetts; Samuel Adams and John Hancock escape arrest, April 19.
1776	Signs the Declaration of Independence.
1783	Treaty of Paris signed. England recognizes the new nation.
1789	Elected lieutenant governor of Massachusetts.
1793	On the death of John Hancock, becomes governor of Massachusetts.
1803	Dies in Boston, October 2.

SOURCE NOTES

Each source note includes the first word or words and the last word or words of a quotation and its source. References are to books cited in the Selected Bibliography.

p. 5   "Every dip . . . horned snake.": Thayer, p. 66.

p. 8   "The value . . . exceeds riches.": Irvin, p. 21.

p. 14   "Taxation . . . tyranny.": Fradin, p. 26.

p. 20   "It is at . . . do not.": Lossing, v. 1, p. 52.

p. 22   "This meeting . . . the country!": Fradin, p. 78.

p. 27   "What a glorious . . . is this!": Lossing, v. 1, p. 52.

SELECTED BIBLIOGRAPHY

Canfield, Cass. *Samuel Adams's Revolution, 1765–1776.* New York: Harper & Row, 1976.

Fradin, Dennis Brindell. *Samuel Adams: The Father of American Independence.* New York: Clarion Books, 1998.

Galvin, John R. *Three Men of Boston.* New York: Thomas Y. Crowell Company, 1976.

Harlow, Ralph Volney. *Samuel Adams, Promoter of the American Revolution.* New York: Holt, 1923.

Irvin, Benjamin H. *Samuel Adams: Son of Liberty, Father of Revolution*. New York: Dial, 1973.

Lossing, Benson J. *Harper's Encyclopedia of United States History*. (10 vols.) New York: Harper & Brothers, 1907.

Thayer, William Roscoe. *George Washington*. Boston: Houghton Mifflin, 1922.

RECOMMENDED WEBSITES

http://www.colonialhall.com/adamss/adamss.php

http://www.whitehouse.gov/kids/dreamteam/samueladams.html

http://www.ushistory.org/declaration/signers/adams_s.htm

http://www.theamericanrevolution.org/ipeople/sadams.asp

http://www.patriotresource.com/people/samadams.html

AUTHORS' NOTES

Samuel Adams was born while England and its colonies were still using the "old style" Julian calendar with a built-in error of one day every 160 years. By 1752, when England adopted the Gregorian calendar, eleven days had already been lost. So September 16, 1722, as Samuel first knew the date of his birth, became September 27, 1722.

Deacon Adams's brother Joseph was the grandfather of John Adams, the second president of the United States, and the great-grandfather of John Quincy Adams, the sixth president.

The name "Sons of Liberty" was coined by a member of Parliament, Colonel Isaac Barre, who predicted that the colonial "sons of liberty" would fight the new tax laws.

At a trial after the Boston Massacre, the British soldiers who fired on the colonists were defended by John Adams and found not guilty on the grounds that they had been provoked and shot into the crowd in self-defense.

Evidence suggests that although Samuel Adams played a major organizational role in the Boston Tea Party, he was not one of the patriots disguised as an American Indian who dumped tea into Boston Harbor.

After signing the Declaration of Independence, Samuel Adams was less involved in politics. He initially opposed the Constitution because he felt too much power was left in the hands of the upper classes. He was pleased when the Bill of Rights was added to protect the rights of the individual.